ALL THINGS NEW

*Rediscovering the
Four-Chapter Gospel*

Hugh Whelchel

INSTITUTE FOR
FAITH, WORK
& ECONOMICS

First Edition, 2016
ISBN 978-0-9964257-9-7

Published by the
Institute for Faith, Work & Economics
8400 Westpark Drive
Suite 100
McLean, Virginia 22102

www.tifwe.org

ALL THINGS NEW

Rediscovering the
Four-Chapter Gospel

CONTENTS

INTRODUCTION

A powerful scene at the end of J. R. R. Tolkien's *The Lord of the Rings* was not in the movie. After the ring is destroyed at Mount Doom and eagles rescue Sam and Frodo, Sam wakes up from his sleep surprised he is alive and surprised to see Gandalf standing at the foot of his bed.

> He gasps, "Gandalf! I thought you were dead! But then I thought I was dead myself. Is everything sad going to come untrue?"[1]

Pastor Tim Keller recognized how deeply Sam's question resonates in the hearts of men and women around the world in his sermon the Sunday after the 9/11 terrorist attacks.[2] Put plainly, the world today does not make sense, especially in the presence of such terrorism. Even with the saving grace of Jesus Christ, the reality of sin makes it plain that things are not as they should be. Pain, suffering, and destruction plague the earth. As Christians, we struggle to find purpose in our work. We face conflict in relationships. We have trouble applying our faith to every area of life. We get stuck in the rut of mundane life, unable to see how the stories in the Bible connect to our day-to-day lives.

The answer to Sam's question can be found in the historical redemptive narrative of the Bible. The Bible begins with, "In the beginning God created the heavens and the earth."[3] This is not only the beginning of the creation story but also the beginning of the "universal story that will ultimately embrace the whole of creation, time, and humanity within its scope."[4] The story ends with the last verse of Revelation.

This way of describing how the Bible is organized is commonly called the **four-chapter gospel:** Creation, Fall, Redemption, Restoration.

- Creation explains the way things were;
- the Fall explains the way things are;
- Redemption shows the way things could be; and
- Restoration shows the way things will be.

The four-chapter gospel is not just a way to read the Bible. It's the framework through which we live our lives. Everyone sees the world through a unique view or perspective, a worldview. As Christians, we see the world through the perspective of the Bible. Think of the four-chapter gospel like a set of prescription glasses that helps us focus our actions and decisions based on God's great story of his creation. When we look at the Bible as one big story and only see two chapters (Fall and Redemption), we miss half the story. Our glasses are a little blurry; things are out of focus. When we live with a blurry prescription for a long time, our eyes adjust. Life out of focus becomes normal, and we struggle to realize we could be seeing something more. With a new set of glasses, everything becomes clearer. The four-chapter gospel is just that – the sharpest, most complete view of life that is true for all of humanity. It serves as the most accurate prescription through which to view and understand the world.

Reading the Bible as one comprehensive story enables us to understand our identity as God's people and to identify our role in his story. From this perspective, we can clearly recognize our call to participate in God's redemptive mission. Our identity as God's people comes from our missional role in the biblical story, which is not in the future but in the here and now. By recovering Scripture's grand story, we fully understand how God calls us to steward all he has given us in every relationship and aspect of our lives. God calls us to himself, but he also calls us to our family, our community, our vocation, and our church. The four-chapter gospel helps explain why we are called to these areas and how we can live out our response to them in light of our love for God. It's the ultimate story of significance for all of humanity.

Scripture opens with the Creation account in Genesis, explaining the beginning of all things. It ends in Revelation with an account of a total renewal and restoration of all of creation. From Genesis to Revelation, the Bible explains all of history. N. T. Wright, a well-known New Testament scholar, says that the divine drama told in Scripture "offers a story which is the story of the whole world. It is public truth."[5] The biblical metanarrative, or the larger over-arching story of Scripture, makes a universal claim of truth for all humanity, calling each one of us to find our place in God's story.[6]

All of life is told and interpreted through a story. The story of the Bible gives context and meaning to all people, places, and things. It answers the questions that plague our hearts: *Why am I here? What is God's purpose for my life? Why is the world so broken?*

In this booklet, we will explore each chapter of God's grand narrative.

REFLECTION QUESTIONS

How do you think your life fits into the stories told in Scripture?

_____

_____

_____

A worldview is a way to look at the world. It's a theory or conception of the world that informs how one lives. What is your worldview? How does your worldview inform the way you live?

_____

_____

_____

Have you heard of the four-chapter gospel? How is this different or similar to your understanding of the gospel?

_____

_____

_____

CHAPTER 1: **CREATION**

There is a start to every story. The first chapter of the biblical narrative, Creation, explains the way things were in the very beginning. Creation marks the beginning of God's love story to his people. Genesis gives us insight into how we were created and what we were created to do.

In Genesis 1, we learn how God fashioned the world to operate in perfect unity, peace, and complete flourishing – what the Old Testament prophets call *shalom*. In the first few verses of the chapter, God worked, molding the universe out of nothing. We learn that God is a maker, a creator, and an artist who takes pride and finds pleasure in his good work. He created the heavens and the earth, and he was pleased. On the sixth day of creation, God created man and woman, the crowning glory of his work, and he fashioned them in his own image (Gen. 1:27). At the end of the day, he saw everything that he had made and declared it "very good" (Gen. 1:31). God looked upon his work with love and delight.

Scripture tells us this repeatedly.

> "But God shows his love for us in that while we were still sinners, Christ died for us" (Rom. 5:8).

> "For God so loved the world, that he gave his only Son, that whoever believes in him should not perish but have eternal life" (John 3:16).

> "See what kind of love the Father has given to us, that we should be called children of God; and so we are" (I John 3:1).

> "We love because he first loved us" (I John 4:19).

Understanding this context for our creation powerfully transforms how we view our purpose in life. God did not create his people to robotically accomplish his goals. Nor did he create them for purposeless existence. Out of his great love for his people, God fashioned men and women as partners in his grand story to carry out his work alongside him and in a relationship with him. This love is unearthly. We see glimpses of it in our relationships with others, but we cannot fully grasp the depth of our Creator's love for us. In the New Testament, the term *agape* refers to God's love for us. *Agape* is the ultimate form of love. It's not sexual or romantic or friendly or brotherly. It is a radical, self-sacrificing, gracious, unmerited, and faithful love, as we see it play out in later chapters of the gospel. God's love for us knows no end. In it, he calls us to partner with him.

How do we partner with God? In Genesis 2:5, we read that there was "no man to work the ground." After God created Adam and Eve, he gave them a specific task: to care for and work the garden (2:15). He charged them to be fruitful, multiply, fill the earth, and subdue it (1:28). This is known as the *cultural mandate*: God's mandate for humanity to build and cultivate. God created us to work. The cultural mandate gives us meaning, purpose, and a job for our time on earth.

The cultural mandate was true for Adam and Eve, and it is still true for us today. Through the cultural mandate, we understand God's mission for his people. Moses, the author of Genesis, is telling his original audience and us as well that humanity's original calling resides in the creation narrative. God created us as co-workers to be in a relationship with him, to rule over his kingdom, and to exercise dominion. As Dr. Michael D. Williams, professor of theology, states, "The gospel call is a redemptive return to the lost and forfeited calling... to bearing God's image in the world, a calling that has never had anything less than the entirety of God's original good creation in view."[7]

The creation account reveals God's magnificent love for us. He shaped us in his image to reflect his glory and charged us with the greatest responsibility of all his creatures, to care for and cultivate his kingdom. In his image, we have the ability and desire to be in relationships and to create. These aspects of God's image undergird our human dignity, desires, and abilities. We often forget that because of God's love for us, he gave us purpose on earth.

In his book *The Mission of God's People*, Christopher J. H. Wright, an Old Testament scholar, explains our mission as God intended it:

When God created the earth, he created human beings in his own image with the express mission of ruling over creation by caring for it – a task modeled on the kingship of God himself. The human mission has never been rescinded, and Christians have not been given some exemption on the grounds that we have other or better things to do.[8]

Wright's point is critical. This is our greatest task. God's purpose for us is to rule. He expressed this intention in the very beginning of time, and it has not changed. Again, Wright states this plainly:

Creation is not just the disposable backdrop to the lives of human creatures who were really intended to live somewhere else, and some day will do so. We are not redeemed out of creation, but as part of the redeemed creation itself – a creation that will again be fully and eternally for God's glory, for our joy and benefit, forever.[9]

Christians don't always see the biblical narrative as the context for purpose in life. In fact, most often Christians miss this point entirely. Dr. Richard Pratt, an American theologian and author, describes the typical vision some people have of "the Christian life," that Jesus "came to forgive our sin, make our souls sparkle, to sprinkle us with peace and joy so we can sprout wings when we die, grab a harp and join the eternal choir."[10] Nothing could be further from the truth. Out of his magnificent love, God has called each of his children from death to life, from darkness into his glorious light, and he has done this for a reason. Part of that reason has to do with what he wants us to accomplish in the here and now.

Even though the Garden of Eden was good and just how God intended it to be, it was not finished. If Adam and Eve had never sinned, they would not have lived in the Garden of Eden forever. Based on the job description given to them by God himself, they would have moved out into the world filling it with God's images and making the earth useful for humankind's benefit and enjoyment. [11]

We, created in God's image, are what J. R. R. Tolkien called "sub-creators."[12] We cannot create something *ex nihilo* (out of nothing), but we are called to create something out of what already exists. The work we are called to accomplish in all we do sustains the mission intended for us, the mission Moses had in mind when he wrote the opening chapters of Genesis.

Moses was preparing God's people for the mission they were created to carry out – the same mission that applies to Christians in the twenty-first century.

REFLECTION QUESTIONS

Why is the chapter of Creation important to the four-chapter gospel? Does it change your understanding of the gospel?

_____

_____

_____

What are the implications of Creation for your life? Consider how purposeful God was in making the earth. How does his intentionality apply to your own life?

_____

_____

_____

You are created out of love and for a purpose. Reflect and pray over this truth.

_____

_____

_____

CHAPTER 2: **THE FALL**

C reation, the first chapter of the gospel, explains where we came from and why. This context for our existence powerfully informs how we live our lives. The second chapter of the biblical narrative, the Fall, accurately describes the way things are. Genesis 3:1-19 makes it clear that because our first parents rebelled against God, we are fallen creatures with a sinful nature that manifests in selfishness, greed, and exploitation (Rom. 5:12). Things are not the way they are supposed to be.

This rebellion of Adam and Eve against God in the Garden of Eden broke the command he had given to them and introduced sin into the world (Gen. 2:16-17). Sin contaminated every aspect of human life and the created order (Gen. 3:7-24). The unity and peace God had woven into his world, shalom, began to unravel. Every part of the created order was damaged; even the environment was altered. Everything was broken, including our relationship with God.

Today, we see the effects of the Fall in every facet of our lives. We seek independence from God and look to idols to fulfill our longings. We experience despair, hurt, pain, sadness, anger, and envy in broken relationships. We toil internally, wrestling with self-doubt, insecurity, pride, and depression. The earth itself aches from the physical effects of the Fall, groaning from famine, drought, floods, and other natural disasters. Sin has touched all aspects of Creation.

Steve Corbett and Brian Fikkert, economics professors at Covenant College, explain this idea of brokenness in their book, *When Helping Hurts,* depicting the devastation of the Fall on all of humanity's relationships:

> Their relationship with God was damaged, as their intimacy with Him was replaced with fear; their relationship with self was marred, as Adam and Eve developed a sense of shame; their relationship with others was broken, as Adam quickly blamed Eve for their sin; and

their relationship with the rest of creation became distorted, as God cursed the ground and the childbearing process...because the four relationships are the building blocks for all human activity, the effects of the Fall are manifested in the economic, social, religious, and political systems that humans have created throughout history.[13]

Corbett and Fikkert illustrate the truth of relationships: sin plagues how we relate to everything and everyone. Nothing goes untouched. Charles Colson and Nancy Pearcey describe it as, "Every part of God's handiwork was marred by the human mutiny. At the Fall, every part of creation was plunged into the chaos of sin, and every part cries out for redemption."[14] In this fallen state, humans are unable to realize the calling that they were made to fulfill. While God designed work as a good thing, sin corrupted it, ensuring that humans toil and sweat in their labor (Gen. 2:19). In response to the brokenness and chaos, we try desperately to break free from the bondage of sin.

Our own brokenness lies at the crux of these broken relationships. We deny what is true: that Jesus Christ is Lord over our lives, deserving of all honor, glory, and praise. Instead, we value other things over him, especially ourselves. We misplace our trust, confidence, and love in ourselves rather than in God. We deny God's truth and adhere to lies. We choose to live in a way that glorifies "me." From that, all relationships suffer. Our wildly misguided perception of truth and value – our sin – taints all our relations.

This is why the Apostle Paul wrote,

> For the creation was subjected to frustration, not by its own choice, but by the will of the one who subjected it, in hope that the creation itself will be liberated from its bondage to decay and brought into the freedom and glory of the children of God.[15]

The Fall left humans in a state of total ruin, incapable of doing anything that pleases God, and to make matters worse, there is nothing anyone can do to reverse its effects (Rom. 3:9-19; 8:7-8). In all the ways that we know things are not the way they should be, our relationship with God is most broken. His very nature is holy and perfect and cannot tolerate the presence of our wretched sin. We cannot fill the void sin has left between God and us. Consequently, we question God. We doubt him and we seek independence from him. We question his love for us and refuse to believe in his goodness. We grasp for control over our lives. God cannot simply turn his head and overlook our rebellion. His nature requires that justice is done.

In this state, all hope seems lost. Thankfully, this is not the last chapter of the gospel, and we experience the depth of God's grace and love for us in the chapters to come.

REFLECTION QUESTIONS

How do you see the effects of the Fall in your relationships? In your work?

_____

_____

_____

When have you acutely felt the depth of your sin? Why?

_____

_____

_____

In light of the Fall, what can we do to mediate so much sin and brokenness?

_____

_____

_____

CHAPTER 3: **REDEMPTION**

The Fall explains why the world groans in the effects of sin. We experience sin in all the relationships of our lives. Thankfully, we have hope in the person of Jesus Christ. The third chapter of the four-chapter gospel, Redemption, gives us a glimpse of the way things could and should be. God did not abandon the human race. He did not leave it to die in the sin and misery that resulted from Adam's original sin. Instead, out of his great love and mercy, God delivered his people from sin and brought them into salvation by grace through faith, administered by his son Jesus Christ. "God shows his love for us in that while we were still sinners, Christ died for us" (Rom. 5:8). In our sin and wretchedness, we deserve death – the penalty for our sin – but instead God graciously gave us the free gift of eternal life through his son, Jesus Christ (Rom. 6:23). And so, we have hope.

We live in this chapter today.

Christ's death paid the price for all of the sin of his children – the past, present, and future. Christ offers us a way to know God by clothing us in his righteousness. God sent Jesus so that we may have access to a restored, redeemed relationship with him. Through Christ's sacrifice on the cross, God adopts us as his children, and we receive the eternal inheritance of Jesus Christ (Eph. 1:5-6; Titus 3:7). Our status with God changes; we are justified by our faith in Jesus. In II Corinthians 5, the Apostle Paul gives a vivid explanation of the power of the Lord's work in our lives when we trust in him. We are no longer defined by our sin; we are defined by Christ's righteousness. In Christ, we are a new creation. Being made new gives us new life, a life in Christ, through which we have a new perspective of hope and the assurance of our salvation.

Although we do not enjoy the perfect conditions of the Garden of Eden as Adam and Eve did before the Fall, God still intends for us to attain a certain measure of wholeness and flourishing. He calls us to repent of sin and live lives that show others the way things could be. We see the remarkable effects of redemption in all our relationships. God gives us foretastes of glory and hope in our lives to show us what is to come when Christ returns. The impact of redemption in our daily lives is not just theoretical; it is practical. In the midst of great hardship and pain, we experience joy, laughter, love, peace, reconciliation, and beauty. We see redemption in relationships repaired, illnesses healed, cities rebuilt. Successful businesses provide goods and services to consumers around the world, promoting flourishing and prosperity. Innovation and technology have changed the global economy, communication, healthcare, finance, and more. Communities come together in the face of tragedy to rebuild, support, and care for one another. By living lives demonstrative of Christ's love, we extend God's redemptive grace to others.

Just as sin affects all of the creation, the redemption found in Jesus' death has the power to redeem all of the creation. Just as his death gives us unmerited access to God, it changes our relationship with the world, and it renews our purpose in life. T. M. Moore, the dean of the Colson Center's Centurions Program, writes of the greater purpose of our calling made possible by the grace of the gospel:

> So the creation has been "subjected to futility," Paul says, and we who have become the sons and daughters of God, who understand His purpose for our work, have been called in our work to repair, renew, and restore the original beauty, goodness, and truth of God... Our work only takes on full significance when we see it in this light, as part of God's ongoing work to bring everything to a higher state of goodness (Rom. 8:28). So no matter what your job, or whatever your work might be, God intends that you should devote your labors to something greater than personal interest, economic prosperity, or social good, alone. God intends your work to contribute to the restoration of the creation, and the people in it, to raising life on this blue planet to higher states of beauty, goodness, and truth, reflecting the glory of God in our midst.[16]

Everything we do advances this higher state of goodness, according to Romans 8:28. This third chapter of Redemption represents the beginning of the restoration and fulfillment of God's original purposes.[17] Those who are redeemed can fulfill their original calling in Genesis – to have dominion over the earth and to create culture. God has uniquely gifted each person to do this, and through redemption, allowed us to fulfill his call even in our sin.

REFLECTION QUESTIONS

What is the hope we have in Redemption? How does Redemption change your relationship with God?

_____

_____

_____

Why is Redemption important in the four chapters of the gospel?

_____

_____

_____

Reflect on how you see Redemption in your life – in relationships, at work, at church, in your community.

_____

_____

_____

CHAPTER 4: **RESTORATION**

I n Creation, we are made in the image of God out of love and for a purpose. In the Fall, sin affects all of life, alienating us from God. In Redemption, we have hope in the death and resurrection of Christ, by God's grace. Restoration, the fourth chapter of the four-chapter gospel, anticipates the coming of the new age when Jesus returns at his second advent and completes the work he started "making all things new" (Rev. 21:5). In Restoration, he will "wipe every tear from their eyes. There will be no more death or mourning or crying or pain, for the old order of things has passed away" (Rev. 21:4). We eagerly await the final chapter of God's story, Restoration, when there will be whole, complete flourishing.

It is in this final chapter that the whole of physical creation will be restored to, as the Bible describes, new heavens and a new earth. There are two Greek words for "new." The first Greek word is *neos,* which means totally new. The second Greek word is *kainos,* which means renewed. Almost every time the Bible uses the word "new" (referencing new birth, new selves, new creation, new heavens and new earth), it uses the Greek word *kainos.* God will not throw away creation but renew it. Albert M. Wolters, author and religion professor, says, "God does not make junk, and he does not junk what he has made."[18] It is part of God's plan and his intention to make right the damage of sin.

The promise of flourishing revealed in the third chapter of Redemption will become a completed reality. During this last chapter, the resurrected followers of Christ will be given authority to rule over the new earth, under the authority of Jesus the King in a new city, the New Jerusalem. Jesus will restore *shalom* to the entire creation, and his people will live with him for eternity on a physical new earth not marred by the curse of sin.

Stop and consider that last sentence again. God's people will live with him forever. Why? Because God loves his people and desires to be in relationships with them for eternity. In Restoration, we will experience the knowledge of God in a way we cannot even imagine today. In restoring all of the creation, God will fully restore relationships. The earth will not bear the natural disasters of sin. Our bodies will not decay and wither. There will be no more tears, strife, and angst in relationships.

As Christians, the resurrection of our bodies that Paul describes in I Corinthians 15 is our great hope. Yet, while we are invigorated by the hope of what Christ has in store for us, Paul reminds us:

> Therefore, my dear brothers and sisters, stand firm. Let nothing move you. Always give yourselves fully to the work of the Lord, because you know that your labor in the Lord is not in vain. (I Cor.15:58)

Restoration gives us immense hope in what is to come and in the significance of our work today. The "work of the Lord" that Paul refers to is what we are called to do in our families, our churches, our communities, and our jobs. God has blessed his people with resources, gifts, and talents. Our job on earth is to steward and manage those resources to his glory. What is done in the here and now, in the third chapter of Redemption, is still important to God. God gives us these resources so that we can fulfill the cultural mandate in this chapter of redemption. While we cannot perfectly maximize all our resources, we can still use them to the best of our ability in a way that honors God. This is good stewardship.

I Corinthians 15:58 indicates that what is done in the Lord is not in vain. N. T. Wright develops this theme in his book *Surprised by Hope*. He writes:

> You are not oiling the wheels of a machine that's about to roll over a cliff. You are not restoring a great painting that's shortly going to be thrown on the fire. You are not planting roses in a garden that's about to be dug up for a building site. You are–strange as it may seem, almost as hard to believe as the resurrection itself–accomplishing something that will become in due course part of God's new world.[19]

Restoration is the restoration of a *city*. It's a symbol of human progress and a hope for our labor to advance God's kingdom on earth now. God has chosen to include his people in this process. The great privilege of collaborating with him motivates excellence in even the most mundane tasks until one day we realize the fullness of God's kingdom when he will make all things new.

REFLECTION QUESTIONS

Why is the chapter of Restoration important? How does it change your view of the gospel?

_____

_____

_____

How does Restoration affect your day-to-day life? How can a good understanding of Restoration change your perspective of work?

_____

_____

_____

After reading about the four chapter of the gospel, what did you learn? Does this framework change your understanding of God's redemptive narrative in Scripture?

_____

_____

_____

CHAPTER 5: **TWO CHAPTERS OR FOUR?**

Most Christians recognize these foundational truths in their faith.

- I am sinful and broken.
- I cannot fix my sin on my own, so I need a savior, Jesus Christ.

This is the most common message of Christianity. The reality of our sin is impossible to ignore. We face the effects daily, even moment by moment. It is readily clear, as much as we might struggle to admit it, that the world needs saving. It is not the way it should be.

These observations are true, but there is more. Recognizing our brokenness and salvation is essential, but it is not enough. It is not the whole gospel. We call this the two-chapter gospel.

Have you ever wondered, *Why am I sinful? What is the point of my salvation? What is God's purpose for my life?* These questions may take different forms, but they tug at the hearts of every human being. We search for purpose and meaning in all that we do, and yet we come up short.

The four-chapter gospel answers questions of meaning, origin, and ultimate purpose. Many Christians today have lost this larger vision told by the Bible. Despite the greatness of the biblical narrative, in the past 150 years, the church in the Western world has looked at the Bible from the limited perspective of two chapters – Fall and Redemption. Pastor and author Tim Keller points out the importance of telling the whole story:

> Some conservative Christians think of the story of salvation as the
> fall, redemption, heaven. In this narrative, the purpose of redemption
> is escape from this world; only saved people have anything of value,

while unbelieving people in the world are seen as blind and bad. If, however, the story of salvation is Creation, fall, redemption, restoration, then things look different. In this narrative, non-Christians are seen as created in the image of God and given much wisdom and greatness in them (cf. Ps. 8) even though the image is defaced and fallen. Moreover, the purpose of redemption is not to escape the world but to renew it... It is about the coming of God's kingdom to renew all things.[20]

While sin and salvation are undeniable realities, they are not the complete gospel. This abridged version excludes God's original plan for his creation, described in the first chapters of Genesis and characterized by *shalom* – universal flourishing, wholeness, and delight. It also leaves out God's future restoration of all things at the end of the age, also characterized by *shalom*. This incomplete story has a number of problems.

It does not tell us about our true destiny. God's design and desire for his people culminates in eternity with him. God delights in his children so much that he sent his only son to die for us. God did not make the ultimate sacrifice only so that our earthly lives may be a little better. He did so to reconcile his children to himself and spend forever with us.

It does not tell us why we were created. Even in the redemption of Christ, we still mess up and sin. We turn away from God and seek independence. In his omniscience, then, why did he choose to save humanity? Because he loves us. The depth of God's love for his people is so grand that in his grace and through our faith in Christ, he forgives our sin and still allows us to steward his creation. Without God's love and Christ's sacrifice, we would have no hope in our work, in our relationships, or in our lives.

It does not tell us about what we were created to do. God charges his people with a grand mission in the very beginning of Scripture. Without understanding the context of our creation and the purpose for our lives here on earth, we significantly misinterpret our relationship with God. We lose direction in our lives and struggle to find fulfillment in our work.

It tends to over emphasize the individualistic aspects of salvation. Salvation becomes all about us. Our salvation in Christ is realized and celebrated in community. As believers, we are integral parts of the body and bride of Christ – the universal, invisible church. A relationship with God is intimate and personal. You cannot save anyone from their sin, only God can. However, we are designed to grow in Christ with others, so that we may sharpen our brothers and sisters in Christ and show Christ's love to the world (Prov. 27:17).

It becomes a gospel of sin management. If we understand the only point of the gospel to be our salvation from sin, we ignore the power of Christ in our lives to truly transform others, the world, and us. We miss the extensive reach of God's grace. We fail to apply God's purpose in creation to our lives and the world around us. Understanding the four-chapter gospel broadens our perspective on God's supremacy and sovereignty. The four-chapter gospel is about more than your sin; it's about knowing your creator, his purpose for you, and your role in his majestic mission for his people.

It creates a sacred/secular divide. Our response to our Father should be unlimited, all-encompassing, and comprehensive; it's not limited to church on Sundays. It should appear in every dimension of life. A two-chapter gospel creates a divide between what is spiritual and what is secular. This divide is responsible for the popular mindset that our relationship with God is compartmentalized to church-related events and activities. Quite the contrary, our response to God should reverberate into every facet of life: at home, at work, in our families, in our communities, and at church. This divide has also perpetuated the lie that working in the church is the only "full-time Christian service." All of life is spiritual, or sacred. There is no inch of creation where Christ does not rule and consequently no dimension of our lives in which he is not present. By demolishing this dichotomy, we realize that God cares about *everything* we do. Our response to his power and glory can come from every thought, word, and action if we steward all we have to his glory and honor. In this, we find fulfillment.

It tends to lead to an escapist view of redemption. This two-chapter gospel portrays salvation only as a bus ticket to heaven. Christians often believe that what they do while they wait for the bus doesn't really matter. This is not what the Bible teaches. If we leave out the first chapter, Creation, we do not know why we were created. If we leave out the last chapter, Restoration, we do not know about our glorious future. Christopher J. H. Wright in his book, *God's Mission: The Key to Unlocking the Bible's Grand Narrative*, summarizes this missional, four chapter biblical narrative as:

> Our committed participation as God's people, at God's invitation and command, in God's own mission within the history of God's world for the redemption of God's creation... This is The Story that tells us where we have come from, how we got to be here, who we are, why the world is in the mess it is, how it can be (and has been) changed, and where we are ultimately going. [21]

By recovering Scripture's storyline, we rediscover our true identity. Only in this larger four-chapter framework can we understand why we are important to God, why our work is important to God, and why he has called us to be good stewards.

We see the way things were supposed to be in the glorious description of humans as the crowning jewel of creation in Psalm 8. David reflects on the creation story in Genesis:

> You have made them a little lower than the angels
>   and crowned them with glory and honor.
> You made them rulers over the works of your hands;
>   you put everything under their feet:
> all flocks and herds,
>   and the animals of the wild,
> the birds in the sky,
>   and the fish in the sea,
>   all that swim the paths of the seas.

Yet, the author of the book of Hebrews, after quoting this passage in Psalms, makes a startling but obvious claim. "In putting everything under them (man),

God left nothing that is not subject to them (man). Yet at present we do not see everything subject to them (man)" (Heb. 2:8). The author is saying that because sin has entered the world, things are not the way they are supposed to be. Man sinned because he wanted to be like God. He did not want to be a steward; he wanted to be the ultimate owner, ruling the world as he saw fit. As quickly as the author of Hebrews states the problem, he states the answer,

> Yet at present we do not see everything subject to them. But we do see Jesus, who was made lower than the angels for a little while, now crowned with glory and honor because he suffered death, so that by the grace of God he might taste death for everyone (Heb. 2:9).

Adam and Eve chose independence from God. They wanted to rule on their own, and we still do today. Despite their disobedience and rebellion, God saved Adam and Eve, and he saved us. Jesus's perfect life, sacrificial death on the cross, and subsequent resurrection restore his people to their place as stewards of God's creation.

In Redemption, we recognize that it is only through the redemptive work of Christ that Christians can fulfill their call to stewardship. God has given us guidelines in the moral law and filled us with his Holy Spirit so that we might begin to do immeasurably more than all we ask or imagine, according to his power that is at work within us (Eph. 3:20). Without the saving grace and power of Christ, we are effortless to please God in the decisions we make. In his power, we can further God's kingdom in the way he intended.

When Jesus walked on the face of this earth, he healed the blind man and he fed the five thousand. But, why didn't he heal all the sick and feed all the hungry? He certainly could have – he is the son of God. Jesus was demonstrating his power and authority on earth, but the framework of the four-chapter gospel highlights another reason. Jesus was physically on the earth in the third chapter of Redemption to show the way things could and should be. When Jesus healed the blind man, he was pointing to a time when no one will be sick. When he fed the five thousand, he demonstrated that there will be a time when no one will be hungry. Jesus was showing that he has the ability to deliver on his promise of new heavens and a new earth. As his disciples, we are to go out into the world and work to bring about flourishing in everything we do, giving those around us the hope of the way things could be.

As Christians, we are called to live lives so transformed by this four-chapter gospel that others will see in it the possibility of their own transformation and the world's. Our encounter with God changes our heart and posture toward him, others, the world, and ourselves. When we encounter the love of our Father, our response of love is undeniable. It motivates our desire to glorify him above all else.

Sam's question, "Is everything sad going to come untrue?" recognizes that the world is a place that is filled with much sadness and cursed by sin. In the final chapter of Restoration, those sad things will be made untrue. The curse will be rolled back. The world will be forever changed. As we read in the book of Revelation:

> Then I saw a "new heaven and a new earth", for the first heaven and the first earth had passed away, and there was no longer any sea. I saw the Holy City, the New Jerusalem, coming down out of heaven from God, prepared as a bride beautifully dressed for her husband. And I heard a loud voice from the throne saying, "Look! God's dwelling place is now among the people, and he will dwell with them. They will be his people, and God himself will be with them and be their God. 'He will wipe every tear from their eyes. There will be no more death' or mourning or crying or pain, for the old order of things has passed away." He who was seated on the throne said, "I am making everything new!"[22]

The grand narrative of the Bible tells of God's plan to take mankind from the garden to the city of God. This city is the New Jerusalem where we will live forever with Christ. This was always the plan, both before and after the Fall.

REFLECTION QUESTIONS

Why does a four-chapter framework change the way we live and work?

_____

_____

_____

What are the major differences between these two perspectives?

_____

_____

_____

Where do you see the secular/sacred divide in your life? What are the effects of it in your life?

_____

_____

_____

CHAPTER 6: **WHY DOES IT MATTER?**

T he four chapters of the gospel narrative give us a more robust understanding of God's plan for creation. A comparison of the four-chapter and two-chapter versions of the gospel illuminates the comprehensive scope of Creation, Fall, Redemption, and Restoration.

So, why does it matter?

Stories universally give context and meaning to all people in all cultures. Today, many narratives compete to explain *why we are here.* In a crowded arena of worldviews and perspectives, the Bible is the ultimate story of significance that applies to all generations in every era. It's an evergreen explanation of truth.

The four-chapter gospel lays a foundation that provides the meaning and fulfillment we seek in life. It gives us the context of our creation, assurance in our future destination, and a picture of God's design – flourishing. Human flourishing explains the goal of God's redemption for us in Christ, who promises us eternal and abundant life. We can grasp, conceptually, God's love and purpose for us. We can understand his design for flourishing. But, how do we seek it? It all begins with relationships.

Relationships and Biblical Flourishing

We are relational because God is relational. Genesis 1:26 explains this when it says, "Let us make man in our image, in our likeness." The orthodox doctrine of the Trinity recognizes that God is one God, co-existing in three distinct persons of the Father, Son, and Holy Spirit.[23] This is taught in Scripture and has been recognized by the church since the second and third centuries. It is also formalized in early Christian creeds, like the Apostles' Creed and the Nicene Creed. The three persons of the Trinity are forever in perfect relationship with each other. There has always been and always will be absolute love, joy, and peace within the Godhead. The very essence of God is relational, and that essential quality has been imprinted on us as humans. We are made to be in relationships with the Creator and his creation.

Relationships form the building blocks of flourishing. Corbett and Fikkert's framework mentioned previously is helpful here. We know the Fall disrupted all of our interactions. In the most basic exchange, relationships touch every aspect of our lives. They provide the context and currency for productivity, connection, and fulfillment. God designed humans to have four types of healthy relationships, all of which were broken at the Fall:

- Relationship with God: This is our primary relationship, from which the other three flow.
- Relationship with self: We have inherent dignity because we are created in God's image, but we should always value God above all things, including ourselves.
- Relationship with others: Corbett and Fikkert write, "We are made to know one another, to love one another, and to encourage one another."
- Relationship with the rest of creation: We are called to be stewards of creation and sustain ourselves through work.[24]

When these relationships are functioning properly, we experience the fullness of life God intended – *shalom*. We were originally created to have peace with God. From this perfectly intimate relationship with God and a heart focused on our Creator would flow the peace in our hearts that we long for and the peace with others we struggle to find. Sin shattered this peace. When we rightly value God over people, things, and ourselves, we have a proper perspective and posture in all relationships. When we live out the original purpose of these relationships, people are able to fulfill their callings to love their neighbor and glorify God through the work they do in their churches, families, communities, and vocations. Just as the distorting effects of sin touch all of life, this gospel framework informs our perspective for all of life as well.

God established these types of relationships in the beginning so that we might rightly glorify him and corporately flourish. When sin entered the world, these relationships were hopelessly corrupted. It is only through the redemptive work of Christ within us, his people, that these relationships are being restored.

Flourishing Requires Fixing Our Broken Relationships. Where Do We Start?

It seems obvious, but sin has detrimentally affected our ability to flourish. The effects of Adam and Eve's sin were not purely individual but corporate, breaking down relationships between themselves and God and others. The original unity between Adam and Eve was broken: fear, distrust, shame, and disunity now entered the relationship. They lost sight of each other as helpers and companions. Although their bodies were alive, something inside of them died. It was an internal death, tainting every aspect of their lives.[25] Where there was once love, trust, and unity there is now only suspicion, distrust, and conflict.

Discord is brought through this now-broken relationship, leading to conflict between brothers, neighbors, cities, and nations. Through the redemptive work of Christ within us, these relationships are restored. Our response to God's saving grace should be willing obedience to his call in our lives, including obedience to the commands that we love and forgive one another.

Jesus taught us that biblical love should be at the center of all our relationships with others, yet we can love only because God first loved us (John 13:34; I John 4:19). It is only through the power of his Spirit working within each believer that we can begin to restore our relationships with others to the way they are supposed to be.

The 2011 Lausanne Confession of Faith and a Call to Action frames our convictions and commitments in terms of love and suggests that as Christians we are taking up the most basic and demanding biblical challenge of all:

- To love the Lord our God with all our heart and soul and mind and strength;
- To love our neighbor (including the foreigner and the enemy) as ourselves;
- To love one another as God in Christ has loved us, and,

- To love the world with the love of the One who gave his only Son, that the world through him might be saved.[26]

We were not made to flourish except in community, and to do that we must restore the broken relationships we have with each other.

Our Call to Relationships

In community we employ our gifts and talents to serve others. We profit from exchanging goods and services. We create Christ-centered community to encourage and sanctify one another while learning more about the character and nature of God. The body of Christ is a network of interdependent relationships, and God is specifically calling us to live out his will in our daily relationships.

In his classic book *The Call*, Os Guinness, author and social critic, suggests that those who have tasted God's grace have been radically transformed and are now open to living lives according to God's design and desire:

> Calling is the truth that God calls us to himself so decisively that everything we are, everything we do and everything we have is invested with a special devotion and dynamism lived out as a response to his summons and service.[27]

Our primary call then is to become disciples of Christ, obeying his ongoing direction in our lives. God is calling every Christian to submit his or her whole life to him. This calling extends to every area of our lives. Guinness goes on to differentiate between our primary and our secondary callings:

> Our primary calling as followers of Christ is by him, to him, and for him… Our secondary calling, considering who God is as sovereign, is that everyone, everywhere, and in everything should think, speak, live, and act entirely for him.[28]

We are God's stewards, given the responsibility to care for and cultivate his earth. Primarily, God designed us to be in an intimate relationship with him and to glorify him in everything we do. He made us with talents and gifts to do that in a way that pleases him. Sin makes this harder but not impossible with the help of the Holy Spirit. God desires us to use our gifts the best we can, making decisions to steward his resources the way he intended and ultimately glorifying him. In doing so, God blesses our obedience to him. When we make bad decisions, misusing God's resources, we encounter frustration, pain, and anxiety because things don't work the way God intended them.

Our primary calling to please and glorify God should always lead to a number of secondary callings: our call to the Church, family, community, and vocation. We discern the difference between our primary calling "to be" and our secondary callings "to do" when we fully integrate God's call into all areas of life.

For followers of Christ, these secondary callings should lead us to our unique life purpose, to use our gifts and abilities to bring about flourishing for God's glory. Understanding our calling is not just about finding purpose in our work but finding purpose in everything we do, understanding that we are on a mission for God.

Living through the Lens of the Four-Chapter Gospel

Claiming the context of our creation, to love God and fulfill his mandate, equips us with a clearer calling in our own lives. Because we are specifically designed to know God and love him, and in response love others and the world we live in, we can faithfully pursue our callings to God's glory with the eternal assurance we have in Christ.

Understanding the way things were, the way things are, the way things could be, and the way things will be gives us the perspective and incentive to fulfill God's purposes – namely, to steward all our resources, talents, and gifts in love to the glory of God. This calling touches every aspect of life and all of our relationships. It frames the way we talk, think, and act. It is completely comprehensive.

N. T. Wright uses the helpful metaphor of a play to explain the authority of the biblical narrative.[29] A similar metaphor helps illustrate the importance of understanding our role within God's larger story. Imagine you uncover a lost manuscript of a Shakespearean play. Upon further reading, you quickly realize it is the greatest play Shakespeare ever wrote. It consists of four acts, each with three scenes. As you read the play, you see that Act III scene iii is missing. It has been destroyed or lost over the years. In order to perform the play as Shakespeare wrote it, you have to rewrite scene iii. But, you can't just make up a scene inconsistent with Shakespeare's style. Instead, you must study the larger story and the playwright to understand what Shakespeare intended. While the other acts are important, without Act III scene iii, the play doesn't make sense.

Today, we are living in Act III, scene iii. In order to live out this scene in God's grand story of creation, we must understand who God is and what he intended for his characters, and we must live out that understanding in every dimension of life. We are waiting for the full resolution of the story, living in Redemption, Act III of the play. This is the greatest story ever told, and we play key characters in the story.

Author and theologian Michael Goheen reinforces the relevance of the gospel narrative:

> The question is not whether the whole of our lives will be shaped by some grand story. The only question is which grand story will shape our lives. For the one who has heard Jesus' call to follow him, the call comes with a summons to enter the story of which he was the climactic moment – the story narrated in the Bible. It is an invitation to find our place in that story.[30]

This is why the four-chapter gospel matters imperatively. It focuses our mission within the context of God's greater mission so that we can live lives in obedience and honor of God. In addition, we have an everlasting, assured hope in the restoration of everything sad in this world. It will come undone in the last chapter when God will make all things new. Through our faith in Christ and the grace of God, we will experience eternal, everlasting flourishing in the presence of our creator. ■

REFLECTION QUESTIONS

How has the gospel influenced your relationships?

_____

_____

_____

Consider the idea of flourishing. Do you see it in your life? What are the circumstances?

_____

_____

_____

How can you apply the principles laid out here to your relationship with God and others?

_____

_____

_____

Have you understood your need for a Savior? Have you trusted Christ for salvation? If no, is it time? Why or why not?

_____

_____

_____

ENDNOTES

1. Tolkien, J. R. R., and Alan Lee. *The Lord of the Rings*. Boston: Houghton Mifflin, 2002.

2. Keller, Timothy. "Truth, Tears, Anger, and Grace." Address, The Church in the City, NY, New York.

3. Gen 1:1

4. Wright, Christopher J. H. *The Mission of God: Unlocking the Bible's Grand Narrative*. Downers Grove, Ill.: IVP Academic, 2006. 71.

5. Wright, N. T. *The New Testament and the People of God*. London: SPCK, 1992. 41-42.

6. Goheen, Michael. "The Urgency of Reading the Bible as One Story in the 21st Century." Lecture, Regent College, Vancouver, November 2, 2006.

7. Williams, Michael D. "First Calling: The Imago Dei and the Order of Creation / The Thistle // Covenant Theological Seminary." The Thistle First Calling The Imago Dei and the Order of Creation Comments. October 09, 2014. https://www.covenantseminary.edu/the-thistle/first-calling/.

8. Wright, Christopher J. H. *The Mission of God's People: A Biblical Theology of the Church's Mission*. Grand Rapids, Mich.: Zondervan, 2010.

9. Ibid.

10. Dr. Richard Pratt

11. Gen 1:28

12. J. R. R. Tolkien

13. Corbett, Steve, and Brian Fikkert. *When Helping Hurts: How to Alleviate Poverty without Hurting the Poor—and Yourself*. Chicago, IL: Moody Publishers, 2012.

14. Colson, Charles W., and Nancy Pearcey. *How Now Shall We Live?* Wheaton, Ill.: Tyndale House Publishers, 2004. 198.

15. Romans 8:20-21 NIV

16. T.M. Moore, "Work, Beauty, and Meaning: A Biblical Perspective on the Daily Grind," October 06, 2006 < www.justicefellowship.org/features-columns/archive/1571- work-beauty-and-meaning> (accessed May 1, 2010).

17. Colson, Charles W., and Nancy Pearcey. *How Now Shall We Live?* Wheaton, Ill.: Tyndale House Publishers, 2004. 194.

18. Wolters, Albert M. *Creation Regained: Biblical Basics for a Reformational Worldview*. 2nd ed. Grand Rapids, Mich.: William B. Eerdmans Pub., 2005. 49.

19. Wright, N. T. *Surprised by Hope: Rethinking Heaven, the Resurrection, and the Mission of the Church*. New York: HarperOne, 2008.

20. Tim Keller, "Our New Global Culture: Ministry in Urban Centers," The Resurgence, accessed May 1, 2010, http://www.theresurgence.com/files/Keller%20-%20Our%20New%20Global%20CultureMinistry%20in%20Urban%20 Centers.pdf. - See more at: http://tifwe.org/resources/the-call-to-creativity/#sthash.wKXEHOxF.dpuf

21. Wright, Christopher J. H. *The Mission of God: Unlocking the Bible's Grand Narrative*. Downers Grove, Ill.: IVP Academic, 2006.

22. Revelation 21:1-5 NIV

23. Adams, Cooper P., III. "Understanding the Biblical Doctrine of the Trinity (Godhead)." January 2014. http://bible-truth.org/Trinity.html.

24. Corbett, Steve, and Brian Fikkert. *When Helping Hurts: How to Alleviate Poverty without Hurting the Poor--and Yourself*. Chicago, IL: Moody Publishers, 2012.

25. Somers, Gayle, and Sarah Christmyer. *Genesis: Part I: God and His Creation Genesis 1-11*. Steubenville: Emmaus Road Publishing, 2004.

26. "A Confession of Faith and a Call to Action." The Lausanne Movement. 2011. https://www.lausanne.org/content/ctc/ctcommitment.

27. Guinness, Os. *The Call: Finding and Fulfilling the Central Purpose of Your Life*. Nashville, TN: W Pub. Group, 2003.

28. Ibid.

29. http://ntwrightpage.com/Wright_Bible_Authoritative.htm

30. Goheen, Michael. "The Urgency of Reading the Bible as One Story in the 21st Century." Lecture, Regent College, Vancouver, November 2, 2006.

ABOUT THE AUTHOR

Hugh Whelchel serves as the executive director of the Institute for Faith, Work & Economics and brings a unique combination of executive responsibility, creative educational administration, and technical innovation from over thirty years of diverse business experience. Almost a decade ago, Hugh stepped out of a successful business career in the IT industry to share his experience of turning around unprofitable companies with Reformed Theological Seminary's struggling Washington, DC, campus where he served as the executive director and guest professor.

In addition to his business acumen, Hugh has a passion and expertise in helping individuals integrate their faith and vocational calling. He is the author of *How Then Should We Work? Rediscovering the Biblical Doctrine of Work*, released in May 2012. Hugh is a contributor to *The Washington Post/On Faith* "Local Leaders" website and has been published on The Gospel Coalition website and *ByFaith* Online. He has also been a guest on Moody Radio Network's "In the Market with Janet Parshall," Salem Radio Network, IRN/USA Radio Network, and Truth in Action Ministries' "Truth That Transforms," and the "Jack Riccardi Show," among other shows.

In addition to serving on the board of several Christian non-profits, Hugh has served as the executive director and board member of The Fellows Initiative, an umbrella organization supporting and establishing church-based Fellows Programs which are designed to help young adults understand God's vocational calling on their lives as they enter their careers.

A native Floridian, Hugh earned a bachelor of arts in sociology from the University of Florida and a master of arts in religion from Reformed Theological Seminary. Hugh and his wife Leslie now live in Loudoun County, Virginia. As an ordained ruling elder in the Presbyterian Church in America, he serves in leadership at McLean Presbyterian Church in McLean, Virginia. In what little spare time he has, Hugh enjoys hiking, golfing, and restoring old sports cars. ■

ABOUT THE INSTITUTE
FOR FAITH, WORK & ECONOMICS

The Institute for Faith, Work & Economics™ (IFWE) is a non-profit, 501(c)(3) Christian research organization committed to promoting biblical and economic principles that help individuals find fulfillment in their work and contribute to a free and flourishing society.

IFWE's research starts with the belief that the Bible, as the inerrant Word of God, provides the authoritative and intellectual foundation for a proper understanding of work and economic truths that, when properly followed, can help individuals, companies, communities, and nations flourish.

IFWE's research is based on three core principles:

- Each person is created in God's image and, like him, has a desire to be creative and to find **fulfillment** using their God-given talents through work.
- All work, whether paid or volunteer, matters to God, and we as Christians are called to pursue excellence throughout the week – not just on Sundays – stewarding all that we've been given for God's glory and for the **flourishing** of society.
- Therefore, we as citizens must promote an economic environment that not only provides us the **freedom** to pursue our callings and flourish in our work but also reflects the inherent dignity of every human being.

Our desire is to help Christians view their work within the bigger picture of what God is doing in the world. Not only do we help Christians find personal fulfillment, but we also help them understand how to better alleviate poverty, address greed, and view possessions properly. With a biblical view of work and economics, we can partner together to be meaningful participants in God's plan to restore the world to the way he intended it to be.

Read more about faith and work by Hugh Whelchel!

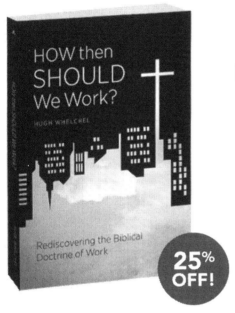

START HERE

The Institute for Faith, Work & Economics provides many resources to help you live a life of freedom, fulfillment, and flourishing. These tools are designed to fit into your life and provide biblical encouragement and guidance to your walk with God.

BLOG
Get our daily or weekly blog updates in your inbox.
BLOG.TIFWE.ORG

RESEARCH
Download free in-depth studies to further your understanding of faith, work, and economics.
RESEARCH.TIFWE.ORG

SOCIALIZE
Connect with IFWE on social media and join the conversation.
FACEBOOK.COM / FAITHWORKECON
TWITTER.COM / FAITHWORKECON

BOOK STORE

Get our latest releases and educational products.

STORE.TIFWE.ORG

DONATE

Become a partner in bringing about flourishing.

DONATE.TIFWE.ORG

PARTICIPATE

Find information about student groups, upcoming events, and other opportunities to get involved.

CONNECT.TIFWE.ORG

INSTITUTE FOR
FAITH, WORK
& ECONOMICS

INSTITUTE FOR
FAITH, WORK
& ECONOMICS

Made in the USA
Middletown, DE
22 April 2016